Sunshine BlackRose

Publications

Melinda Smith

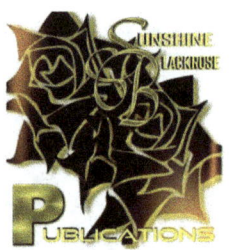

Venting For Release
Expressions of a Sleepless Mind

Melinda Smith

South Carolina

Copyright © 2018 by Melinda Smith.

Published by Sunshine BlackRose Publications
928 Shearwater Way, Warrenville, SC 29851
www.SunshineBRPublication.com

All rights reserved. Printed in the United States of America. No part of this book may be used or reproduced, stored in a retrieval system or transmitted in any manner whatsoever without written permission. The only exception is brief quotations in printed reviews.

Couver design by Clash Custom Designs

ISBN: 978-1-7321910-0-6

CONTENTS

	Introduction	vii
1	Who is Melinda	11
2	Mad at the World	19
3	Self Reflection Self Realization	25
4	My Opinion	35
5	Encouragement	43
6	Just a Little More of Me	53
7	My Joy, My Strength, My Peace	59
	Benediction	63
	Acknowledgements/Dedication	65
	About the Author	67

INTRODUCTION

I'm a very private person, I'm not good at sharing so when it was prophesied to me that I would write a book I brushed it off. "Don't nobody want to hear what I got to say. What would I say anyway?" Those were my thoughts to myself.

I started going over my journals and the poetry I wrote and realized, "Girl you are an emotionally angry person". I am a crazy emotional. Until I reread the stuff I wrote. I couldn't believe just how angry and emotional I was. Key word…WAS

Through my writing I realized the power of forgiveness and letting God do what He does and how he has never left me nor forsaken me.

I also recognized my calling. I am a Phoenix Risings from the ashes. (Isaiah 61:3) I am suppose to reach the broken, the heartbroken, and the hurt. My life, though it's through poetry is a living breathing testimony of survival, perseverance, and God's grace and mercy. How I have walked through the fire sweating and blessings kerosene. I have risen from the ashes several times and God has always provided me with beauty.

I pray that through this book that someone else can learn the power of forgiveness, to never give up, and to trust God always.

Melinda Smith

Venting For Release

Expressions of a Sleepless Mind

Melinda Smith

Chapter 1
Who is Melinda

Melinda Smith

I AM

Who am I?
Well let's see I know I'm not who I use to be
The suburban princess who sought life in the hood
trying to be bad and still be good
Born to a strong willed but bitter single mother
Who kept me in line most of the time when she wasn't
dealing with my gang banging brother
Sweet innocent face on the outside
But hell was living on the inside
Visions of chalk body outlines flooded my mind
The torment was real suicidal contemplations
I just didn't understand the situations
Verbal constipation
Confusion and chaos I just couldn't get it out
Mad at my dad for living at the crack house
Mad at my mom for being blind to my emotional abuse
Mad at any and everybody for not coming to my rescue
Married to a pedophile couldn't believe in such deceit
15 plus years but I just didn't see it
DEFEATED
I felt no love being fat, black, and living in poverty
So I hustled and tried not to let that bother me
I just wanted someone to see the best in me
BITTERNESS towards EVERYBODY
I was lost didn't know what to do with myself
I had to tell myself it's not you it's everybody else
Who am, I why am I here
FEARS
Are things in my life as it really appears
Homelessness, depression, abandonment,
Self-esteem so low
PRIDE high
Alone but not alone, hiding couldn't let it show

Melinda Smith

I talked to doctors who just wanted to medicate
All I wanted was the voices in my head to vacate
Talking all at once they wouldn't be quiet
Maybe I'll try to take myself self out again
Then I'll have some silence
Who am I, why am I here
But this time the voice was different whispering in my ear
He said you are mine and I will see you through
I said, "Well, and you are?"
-I am the great I am I who created you
Where have you been why haven't I heard you before
You were focused on the wrong thing which was your choice
But I had to get your attention so you could hear my voice
Remember when you were brain dead for 3 minutes
You laid on my shoulder and cried because I told you it was not your time
My child listen everything you went through I allowed, it was part of my master plan
And soon you will understand I AM HE who is the GREAT I AM
He said I was his I was intrigued I wanted to know just who THE GREAT I AM was to me
SO I pushed and pressed through the hardship heartache and pain
I labored I suffered I lost everything
I studied it was not in vain when I realized the GREAT I AM is my FATHER'S name
I know my purpose I now know why I am here
The journey has been hard but now I have no fear
WHO AM I
My name has been changed I've become stronger
I know who I am
I am more than a conquer

Venting For Release

I am a vessel used for his purpose
I am His humbled servant
I am his mouth piece
To preach and teach his children
I am fearfully and wonderfully made
I am one in a trillion
I am the daughter of the most high GOD used for his Glory
I am walking in my calling
I am telling my story I am soldier
I am a survivor
I am no longer hiding because of his power
I am a miracle
I am not the same
I am a living breathing testimony
I AM SAVED

Melinda Smith

NOTHING ELSE TO DO

Hurt pain, imagine it
Betrayed shame abandonment
To walk in my shoes most couldn't handle it
Ups and down and the in between
Homelessness living on the streets
Pillar to post
My pride was high I didn't want no one to know
I'm ok everything is fine
No one could tell I was losing my mind
Along with everything else I worked hard for
Twice divorced
I was basically going door to door
Saying I need a place to stay
So many doors slammed in my face
Me and 3 kids living in a car
Money was short so we couldn't go far
Where we could go it wasn't for long before something
in that household went wrong
Trying to quote scriptures to fit the occasions
Jesus I'm tired of being in these situations
I've done all I could for as long as I could
I'm tired of being misunderstood
Trying to figure out what I did
Trying to provide stability for my kids
I was already low no place to go but on my knees
pleading to my father please rescue me
You are all I have there is nothing left in me
My soul ached my spirit slowly dying
My tears fell I'm so tired of crying
Emotionally abused, scared, broken, and defeated I felt
I had nothing left to believe in
No hope no way out but to end it
Couldn't figure out how to believe again

Venting For Release

Out of the mouths of babes the word transpired
Mom God is our provider
Those 4 words got me back on track
And reminded me God has my back
So I have to push on I have to make it through
I have people watching so I gotta do what I gotta do
To hear your child give your own word back to you
"mom you said you can do all things through Christ who strengthen you"
To hear your child say this is going to be one fire hot testimony sitting in the car eating cheese and baloney
You have no choice but to keep going

Melinda Smith

Chapter 2

Mad at the World

Melinda Smith

REVENGEFUL THOUGHTS

Broken heart encased in reinforced titanium steel
Impenetrable unable to heal
Why pray for the hurt to end Just to have it broken again
Wise words once quoted to soothe the soul
Only makes it black and sink into a deeper hole
So it begins
Retaliations seems imminent
An incognito strike to bury those who hurt me in cement
Hoping they drown in the hurt betrayal and pain.
Karma that's her name
My best friend and she's a force to be reckon with
She don't play
I hope I get to see the look on their face
Cold calculating evil way of thinking
You get what you sow
Now it's time for reaping

Melinda Smith

BE AFRAID

Mind spinning out of control
I have lost hold
Riding the waves of this emotional kaleidoscope
There is no hope no more being nice
Wicked witch of the west, heart filled with ice
Words cut to the core
The filter is gone
Tried to keep it in but it's a new dawn
Tired of it all
It's a new me
Prepare for your downfall
I am not who I use to be
You don't have to like it
I really don't care
You're probably one of the ones who took me there
Why be scared
Why be afraid
Of the monster you helped create
Equipped to put the fires out in hell
I don't need a rida
I am a one woman Cartel

CONTEMPLATION OF THE KILL

Idle time cause calculating minds to contemplate how to take out the enemy.
There's two sides from which I can ride trying not to let the evil get the best of me.
My angel side is saying play nice but that evilness is talking slice and dice throw the pieces to the wolves.

The battlefield is set but the entrance is yet to be determined.
Blue prints drawn but yet to be executed.
Got to play this game correctly to much collateral damage at stake.
Need to infiltrate the enemy's mind from within to cause the most limited amount of damage as possible if possible
Sneak attack or full on frontal
The armor is titanium reinforced steel and indestructible
Weaponry is high tech and loaded
Snipers set
Head in the crosshairs
Tic toc tic toc game on

Melinda Smith

Chapter 3

Self Reflection
Self Realization

Melinda Smith

THE FACTS

Out of character not myself
Feeling like I'm somebody else
Dishonest Lying Stealing Making bad choices
If I was crazy Id blame it on the voices
But I'm not it's me
That other side I didn't want to see
The one when pushed would do things by any means necessary
I tried to keep her hidden, locked in a cage
But times come when you unleased the beast and let loose the rage
The pendulum broke and now I can't contain her
She does things fast, it's a flash…a blur
And her work is done, deed completed
Not for glory, not for fame just to the family maintained.
The gotta eat, so think quick and be fast on your feet
Ugh!
I gotta get control let go and give God back the control
When did I let go of His hand
I just don't understand
When did I get into this circumstance
I can see the new beginnings but it's just out of reach
Times are hard and I'm feeling the heat
Can't cry cause I don't feel sad
Frustrated, upset, disappointed, and mad
I know I'm supposed to be better, know better
Do better
But I just can't get it together

Melinda Smith

HELP ME LORD

So many nights have I cried
I'm dead but cannot die
I'm alive but cannot live
Taken advantage of the more I give
My heart broken into so many pieces
The smile I have is facetious
It hides unbearable emotional scars
Trying not to become cold and hard
Bitterness creeping in like a thief
Trying to hold on to my belief
That trouble doesn't last always
His righteous he doesn't forsake
I'm trying to live holy
Not to let life to get the best of me
That this is not my reality
This test I didn't study for
I'm determine not to fail anymore
I need to pass and move on to the next level
But this damn devil and his shovel
I need to come out of this sinking sand
I'm drowning I can't reach you hand
I see you but do you see me
Screaming
Yelling
Help please rescue me
Where are you
I can't feel you here
You leaving me is the worst of my fears
Lord, I can't do this by myself
JESUS MY GOD I NEED YOUR HELP

ESCAPE

Internal discussions on the verge of eruption can cause disruption of peace
But I gotta get it out
Principles and variables can change the scenarios of situations that never seem to cease
But I gotta get out
Overly thinking, the feeling of sinking, not knowing which way to go can cause an increase of wanting to escape
I really need to get out
I need a place when the sound of alarm indicates harm from Satan's charm
I need to get out
Imploding explosions of internal corrosion on my mind that
I can never seem to get out
Precession decision may cause a division amongst the citizens
But I really need to get out

Melinda Smith

RISE ABOVE IT ALL

You can take me as I am
Flaws and all
Or you can walk away and leave me alone
I'm perfectly imperfect
Head high standing strong
I live my life to please no man but God
He's my only judge and jury he has put no fear in me
Therefore, I see things clearly
My future is that of envy
You can't be me or takeaway what God has for me
My haters are my motivators
Making me a better innovator
Rising to the top like an elevator
Up in the clouds
The impact I make
LOUD
Sonic boom
Blasting in your ear like a stereo
Food for thought type of material
Soothing to you soul
Better then honey nut cheerios
The path I walk only God knows
Tough roads ahead but as God as my head
I have no problem being led
To my destination
To my destiny
With God by my side I take it all in stride
Because he only wants the best for me
What better father can you ask for who encourages you
to want more out of life
To leave a legacy for all generations
Leaving a guide, a foot print for all to see
I'm proud that He's making an example out of me

Melinda Smith

Trials and tribulations has made me strong
I cried but after I internalized
I moved on knowing the storms wouldn't last long

UNDERSTANDING

So lost so confused my life feels like
I'm wearing two left shoes
My head hurts
My heart aches
My soul thirst
Trying to find my way
God's time is not my time
But my patience is on a thin line
I know that's the lesson
I've yet to learned
And the sooner I do
Maybe the pages will turn

Melinda Smith

LETTING GO

Out of sight out of mind
Doesn't always work when the souls are tied
God ordained true love to stand the test of time
And beat the Odds
A roller coaster ride of up and down happiness
Sadness, joy, and pains
You either change or remain the same
You fight a good fight and stay in the race
You compromise and communicate
Sometime you grow in different directions
You just grow apart
Doesn't mean you are not in my heart
You just can't go
Where God is taking me

Chapter 4
My Opinions

Melinda Smith

DON'T COME FOR ME

Don't care how you feel
Don't care what you think
The bottom line is
I keep it real
I don't pretend to be perfect
I fall short everyday
But I say what I mean and I mean what I say
2 Timothy 2:15
Do your best to present yourself to God as one approved
A worker who has no need to be ashamed
Rightly handling the truth
The way I look to you is not how God sees me
I will do His will by any means necessary
I will talk the way I need to
And go where it's not pleasant
To win souls and get us into heaven
Whether it's businessmen, doctors, and lawyers
The trap house or your house
I AM HIS SOLDIER
I AM HIS WARRIOR
I go where He sends me
To speak His Word
That will set the captives free
UNDETERRED
UNFAZED
UNASHAME
ALL IN JESUS NAME
My way to speak, preach, and teach
May be unorthodox
If it encourages and edifies
I will not be put into a religious box
The world has changed

Melinda Smith

His Word is the same
But you can't save the masses like the ole days
You have to be on your game
You have to reach them where they are
On their level
If the end result is finding their salvation
I'll do whatever to teach them to resist the devil
I don't have it all
I've taken a lot of lost
My life is a testimony for the man who died on the cross
For that sacrifice I owe Him everything
Don't judge the road I'm traveling
As long as He is pleased
Your thoughts and opinions mean nothing
Roman 14:13

HAVE YOU NOT MET ME

I trust you as far as I can spit
Cotton mouth
Everybody suspect
Nobody is legit
How about
I exit stage left
To the left
Left you speechless
Cause you thought I was always going to be there
When you needed me
Believe me
I did to
But the deceptions became apparent
When I couldn't do what I do
Fair exchange is no robbery
Now watch me do what I do
And get your feelings hurt
And when I finish flipping the script
The work will be well worth it
Because you deserve it
Bury your ass like a dead monkey from the circus

Melinda Smith

THE AUDACITY

Who are you?
To question my integrity
Who are you?
To question my character
What is the truth of the lies you believe
And to you what does it matter?
Who are you to judge my mistakes?
If I fall short of HIS GLORY does that make me fake?
Who are you to throw stones?
What about the sins you own?
Who are you to pass judgement?
With you I have no covenant
I didn't know you owned heaven and hell
Is this the love of God?
I can't tell
His word says loves covers a multitude of sin
But the way the world is the enemy is a friend
Disguised as a friend
Where's the love then?
Who are you cause you're not who you say you are?
What's really in your heart?
Has it been there from the start?
Curious minds want to know
Are you filled with a fake Holy Ghost?
Who are you?
Examine yourself
Before your begin to speak on someone else
The same judgment your speak on me
Will be the same judgement you get
When it's your turn in the seat

TEMPTED NOT TEMPTED

Real life strife with headaches and heartbreak trying too hard to stay focused and concentrate
Vindicate and balance life situations
With the Word of god to life applications
The bigger picture is hazy
I think I'm going crazy
Twilight zone
Holy hoes
Financial pot holes
Opposition resistance
Fighting for my life
Trying to live right
But the dark side calling is insistent
Persistent
The dramedy of life
I love you but I love somebody else too just don't sound right
This is history on repeat
#2 or #3
Being anything other than #1 won't do for me
If you can't choose
I'll do it for you
Fall back fade to black is what I'll do
Feeling tucked so deep
Poseidon trident couldn't find them
I laugh to hide the pain
But it's not really comedy just insane
Mind control bondage manipulation
Love with stipulations
But you a Christian......side eye

Melinda Smith

Chapter 5

Encouragement

Melinda Smith

IT'LL BE WORTH IT

Complete restoration takes time it takes patience
It takes forgiveness it takes love
It takes complete and total faith in the father above
Sometimes it's instantaneous
Sometimes months
Sometimes years
But you have to know that it will be worth the pain and
worth the tears
All the fears
All the struggle
All the heartache
Is not in vain
Nothing ventured
Nothing gained
Anything worth having is not easily obtained
Smile to hide the pain beneath the surface
Because in the end
It will all be worth it

Melinda Smith

WARNING WARNING

Turbulence
Incorrect flight patterns
Keep going in circles like the rings of Saturn
This is torturous
Danger Danger
Will Robinson
Spinning Spinning Spinning
Houston we have a problem
Looking for a landing pad
I keep telling myself it can't be this bad
Is this a nightmare or virtual reality?
Caught in the matrix where's the control ALT delete
I got to get out, gotta change the scenery
Trapped in my mind and no one is hearing me
Or seeing the torment of the past cycles repeating
Tired of this class
Where my Bible
I need a Word or 3 or 4
My body hurt
My mine is sore
I can't change the channel the noise in my head
I would press mute but the batteries are dead
JUST LIKE ME
If you don't get it together and stop being lazy
Warning comes before destruction
Time for mental reconstruction
Open your word
Psalms 91 or Psalms 23
Philippians 4:13
I can do all things through Christ who strengthens me
Focus on the voice and the noise
Any promise He's made will not come back void
He's the conductor, the counselor, the pilot and the

Melinda Smith

Bouncer
Our mind He controls, holds, guides, and oversees, and
Fight battles we don't always see
Whatever is invading you mentally, physically,
Spiritually, financially, or emotionally
Is not from God or an already defeated enemy
Sometimes it's you
Get out of yourself and everybody else and get in
GOD
He know what to do

REMEMBER

Trying to cope with this emotional kaleidoscope Life
Lessons
Pain
Hurt
Betrayal
Rejections
You win some
You learn some
Abandoned there is no one
Hard to trust anyone
Forgiveness they say is the key
7 times 70
I die daily
I know He saves me
Roman 8:17
To get the glory we must endure suffering
He's been through what we are going through
No matter how minimal
No matter the issue
He is with you
In His word there is evidence
On How to upgrade your confidence
When you've been let down or you feel like a reject
I encourage you to think back
Jesus Christ paid the price
To give you eternal life
So what can a man do to you

Melinda Smith

WHAT IS LOVE

Love covers a multitude of sin when used correctly
Directly affecting a life change
Healing hurt and healing pain
No shame
Love can bring a smile to people faces
Helping them to see the light in dark places
No condemnation
Pulling them out of pits of despair
By knowing that someone really cares
But be ware
There are different levels of love
Some are small gestures and some go beyond and above
Love is not wanting anything in return
Love is given freely not earned
Love protects covers and hides
Love is patience
Love is kind
Love is used to edify
Love is forgiving and understanding
Love is joy and happiness
Love is a commandment
Simple yet complex
Love has a lasting effect
Expect
Love to life your spirits and sooth the soul
Love is the greatest story ever told
What greater love is there then sacrifice
For a man who has no sin to be nailed to the cross to die
That's the love Jesus has for you and I

EMBRACE THE CHANGE

Change of Name
Change of Heart
Change of Location
A fresh start
To become different
Become something else
Metamorphosis of oneself
Emerging from a cocoon
Spread your wings and fly
The time is opportune
For a change of direction
A shift into a better position
Reflection
Ignore the rejection
Resurrection
Modification
Another phase
Transition
Transformation
An essential stage
Be strong be courageous
Do not be afraid or terrified because of change
Remake
Remodel
Leave the old at the alter
Revise
Redo
Upgrade to the new improved you
Mind soul and spirit is renewed
You will not be the same once you
Embrace the change

Melinda Smith

WAYWARD SOUL

Pressing through the pain of growth
The seed within you, it's breaking through
Each petal that blossoms will speak truth
Strength, courage, perseverance
The heart of a warrior
Champion spirit
Oh wayward soul
Don't give up now
So close to the goal
Things are about to turn around
The SON is shining down
Embrace the feeling
The ending of a thing
Is just the start of a new beginning

Chapter 6

Just a Little More of Me

Melinda Smith

HOLY GHOST HIGH

Peer pressure to take a hit
I was scared what is this
Nah, man I'm good
I'm not into that
So I took a step back and I pushed it away
I'll try it later you know one day
The offer appeared once again
I got curious cause it was changing my friends
But not in a bad way
Their lives were improving
I thought maybe this is something you should be doing
A positive influence
So I indulged and inhaled deeply
The euphoria I felt completed me
I never felt like this before
When I woke up I was on the floor
In a dazed completely amazed
This is something I need every day
Man!
How much does this drug cost?
I'd spend my last dime
And I would stay high all the time
Sell my soul for one more hit
I'm feigning
Withdraw symptoms
I need it
Well they don't sell it on the streets
It's free
All you have to do is sell out to Christ

Melinda Smith

Completely
I am so glad I gave in
I am so glad I tried
My name is Melinda
And
I'm addicted to the Holy Ghost high

Venting For Release

LIFE ACTION CAMERA

Even tho it looks like what it seems
It ain't what it is
Many scenes to a movie still being written
Plot
Twist
Schemes
Turns
Secret messages
Hidden Screams
Cries and laughter
The innocent look of the backstabber
The crooked grin of a friend of a friend
The enemy of my friend is my friend
Fake high fives
How will the story end
Everybody plays a part
Nice guy vs bad guy
In this heart to heart
Action
Drama
Comedy
Horror
Biography
History
Documentary
Who done it mystery
Love story
Made for TV movie
Reality show
Called life
Award worthy

Melinda Smith

Chapter 7

My Joy, My strenghth, My peace- My Boys

Melinda Smith

FOR MY MEN

I shed a tear for you when you can't cry for yourself
I'll be there for you when you have nobody else
I'll be that listening ear for you when you need someone to really hear
I'll be with you when you have to face your fears
I'll burn down a path for you when you feel surrounded
I will breathe for you when you feel like you're drowning
I'll be the peace when you feel like you're at your wits end
I'll rejoice with you in every victory you win
Though good and bad, highs and lows
I'll be with you where no one else will go
I'll hold your hand, push you back, or pull you through
No matter what I'm always going to be with you

RIDE OR DIE-STRONG FAMILY

Melinda Smith

OUT OF THE MOUTHS OF BABES- THINGS MY CHILDREN HAVE TOLD ME

You never Know who you're supposed to be if you are walking with people who don't know who they are or where they're going.-Dre

Bless those who can't help themselves and a better blessing will come upon you-Mykel

Embrace your pass while living in the present in preparation for your future- Mykel

Your opinion is not fact. It just means you feel a certain way about what we are talking about. Therefore I don't have to agree with it because you feel like that. I need concrete evidence for your opinion to be fact in my life-Matthew

Benediction

Struggles should not replace the smile on your face
Count it all joy
Remember Job, everything was taken away
You have to release to be renewed
It only means
God, the universal creator has put trust in you
So much so because of your faith
No matter how dim or grim
Remove negative people and perceptions
Count on divine spiritual protection
When GOD's hands are on you
You're unstoppable
The greater later will be remarkable
Keep your head up and stand strong
Trouble doesn't last long
Get out of your own way
Faith will get you there
Push-Press-Pray

Melinda Smith

I will never admit that I'm lonely
I will never admit that I'm stressed
I will never admit that I'm worried
Or that scared is the S on my chest
I will never admit sometimes
I like trash or just a piece of ass
I will never admit the tears that are there behind the mask
I will never admit I feel lost
I will never admit I lost or failed
I will never admit I need help
I WILL ADMIT
I handled it like a boss
And
I survived hell
My smile is genuine
My heart is pure
Even after the pain and heartache I endured
Giving up is not what I do
Warrior Soldier
I'm living proof
You can survive anything
And that's the whole truth
And nothing but the truth

ACKNOWLEDGMENTS/DEDICATION

I would like to start off by thanking Clash Custom Designs for my book cover, Blacktopia Advertisement for helping with the promotion of my book, and last but not least Sunshine BlackRose Publications for connecting me with these people and putting it all together.

To each and every minister, apostle, prophet, and pastor that has taught me and imparted into my life I thank you from the bottom of my heart.

I dedicate this book to my mom Leila. Your strength resides in me. I don't know a stronger person and I'm grateful for everything you taught me. I love you Chuck, you don't do sappy but just know I love you and thanks for always having faith that I can do it. To all my brothers (to many to name) that have adopted me along that way, thanks for holding me and the boys down. Good looking out y'all are the real MVPs… lol

I dedicate this book to my sisters, Alicia, Demetrice, Aliscia, Vera, and especially Nikki, my own personal 5 fold ministry. Thank you for correcting when I'm wrong, supporting me, and pushing me always to be and do better. Thank you ladies for never hesitating to always keep it real with me. I have plenty others I call my sisters that I didn't name I love you all as well. It's just too so many of you to name, so if I've ever called you my sis I'm talking to you.

Melinda Smith

I dedicate this book to the following, you know who you are:
M.E., A.K., T.K., T.M. W.S., and A.B.
I swear if your guys hadn't pushed me to the point of no return I would have never known my calling. I thank you and love each and every last one of you.

I dedicate this book to my children Mykel, Matthew, and Andre. If God had not blessed me with you three I wouldn't have survived half the things we went through. You guys held me together when I wanted to fall apart. I will always be ride or die for you. I love you.

Finally, I dedicate this book to my Lord and Savior, Jesus Christ. For without You, God I have nothing.
I am nothing.
I owe you my life.

THE AUTHOR

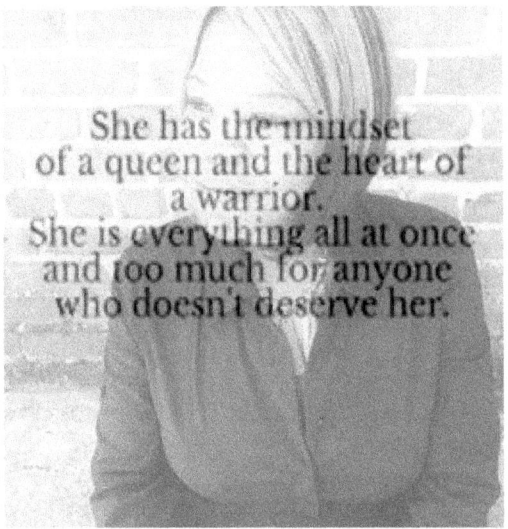

Melinda Edenburgh Smith is the mother of three boys Mykel, Matthew, and Andre. Melinda was born and raised in Cleveland, Ohio and currently resides in Atlanta, Ga.

She is a prolific writer, spoken word artist, mentor, life coach, intercessor and worshipper that truly has a big heart and a love for God's people.

CEO and founder of Phoenix Risings Enterprises, which includes her tax preparations and credits repair business. Melinda's motto is "Rise, Rebuild, Restore" which is based on Isaiah 61:3.

God will give you beauty for your ashes.

Melinda Smith

www.ingramcontent.com/pod-product-compliance
Lightning Source LLC
Chambersburg PA
CBHW052116070526
44584CB00017B/2518